Seth and Sara Ask...

Does God Love
Michael's Two Daddies?

Written by Sheila K. Butt
Illustrated by Ken Perkins

APOLOGETICS PRESS

Seth and Sara Ask...
Does God Love Michael's Two Daddies?

Copyright © 2006 by Apologetics Press

All rights reserved. No part of this book may be reproduced in any manner whatsoever without written permission from the publisher, except in the case of brief quotations in articles and reviews.

ISBN-10: 0-932859-94-1
ISBN-13: 978-0-932859-94-5

Library of Congress: 2006924607

Written by Sheila K. Butt

Illustrated by Ken Perkins
Cover by Charles McCown

Printed in China

Dedication

This book is dedicated to my grandchildren and to parents who truly desire to bring their children up in the "nurture and admonition of the Lord" (Ephesians 6:4).

Apologetics Press

230 Landmark Drive

Montgomery, Alabama

36117-2752

www.ApologeticsPress.org

Seth and Sara are twins. Today is their first day of school. The school building looks so big. They wonder if they will get lost in there. They are excited about meeting new friends.

When Seth and Sara get to their classroom they join a boy named Michael at the puzzle center. The pieces of the puzzle are very big. "This is the biggest puzzle I have ever put together!" said Michael.

"Look," said Sara. "There is a mom and a dad in the puzzle. And two children are riding in the back seat. That looks like our family."

"Yes," said Seth. "It looks like they are going on vacation."

Michael frowned. "My family doesn't look like that," he said. "I have two daddies."

Sara's eyes widened. "Do you have two mommies, too?" she asked.

"No," Michael said. "Just two daddies."

"Where is your Mom?" asked Sara.

"I'm not sure," said Michael. "But I heard my two daddies talking about getting married. They asked me if I would like that. But I don't know if I would or not."

Now Seth and Sara were confused. They did not know how Michael could have two daddies and no mommy. And they did not know if two daddies could get married!

At the end of the day Seth and Sara's mother came to pick them up. On their way out to the car, they saw Michael riding home on the bus. They waved good-bye to their new friend. Seth and Sara couldn't wait to sit down with their parents at dinner and tell them all about their first day of school.

That evening after Dad had said the blessing at the dinner table, Seth remembered what Michael told them at school.

"Guess what! Michael has two daddies," Seth exclaimed. "I didn't know you could have two daddies!"

Seth's Dad looked at him. "Does he live with both of his daddies?"

"Yes," said Seth.

"He even heard them say they wanted to get married," Sara told her Mom.

"Can two daddies get married?" asked Seth.

Genesis

In the beginning
GOD created th
Heavens

Daddy looked serious now. He wanted Seth and Sara to understand what the Bible says about marriage. He wanted them to understand how important it is to obey God.

"Do you remember when we read in the Bible about the beginning of the world?" he asked Sara and Seth. "God decided to make a man and a woman."

"Yes," said Seth, "That was Adam and Eve."

"That's right!" Dad said. "And they were the first husband and wife."

Did He make two men to be married?" asked Dad.

"No," said Sara.

"Did he make two women to be married?" asked Mom.

"No," said Seth.

"That's right," their father said. "But in this world there are some men who want to live together like they are married. And there are some women who want to live the same way. But from the beginning of time, God planned for a man and a woman to be married."

"So Michael's two daddies are not doing what God says, are they Daddy?" Seth asked.

"No," Dad replied. "And when we do not do what God tells us to do, we are sinning. Do you both understand what sin is?" He asked.

"Yes," said Sara. "Sin is doing something wrong. It is not obeying God."

"The Bible tells us not to sin," added Seth.

"And if we do sin, we have to make it right in order to be pleasing and acceptable to God." Mother said. "We have to repent. That means we have to turn away from the wrong we are doing and do what the Bible says is right."

"So that means that Michael's two daddies should not get married, doesn't it Daddy?" Sara asked. "It means they should not live together like a husband and wife."

"That is exactly what the Bible teaches," Dad said.

"Does God love them anyway?" asked Seth.

"Yes," Dad replied. "God loves them. He sent His Son to die on the cross for them, too, just like He did for you and me. And we need to make sure that we love them just like God does. But since Jesus gave His life for our sins, God expects us not to sin. If we are doing something wrong we must stop if we want to be a child of God—a Christian. We must repent if we want to be a part of the body of Christ."

"Let's see if you two know what the body of Christ is," Dad asked.

"I know," beamed Sara. "It's people in His church who love Jesus and obey His words in the Bible!"

"You are right," Dad said. "And when Jesus comes again, the Bible says He is going to take His body, the church, to heaven to live with God."

"I want to go to heaven!" smiled Sara.

"Me, too!" said Seth.

"Your Mother and I want both of you always to do what the Bible teaches," Dad said. "We hope our whole family can teach others what the Bible says so they can be in heaven, too."

"I like Michael," Seth said. "I am going to invite him to come to Bible class with me this week."

"That's a great idea! I hope he can come," Mother added, smiling. "In the meantime, we have to practice your reading words. Won't it be wonderful when you two can read the words of the Bible for yourselves."

— *Scripture References* —

Genesis 2:21-24

Matthew 19:4-6

Mark 10:6-9

Romans 1:26-27

1 Corinthians 6:9-11

1 Timothy 1:9-11

Acts 17:30-31

John 3:16-17